I Was There

DAVID E. RIDENHOUR

A
Good Friday
Tenebrae
Service

C.S.S. Publishing Co., Inc.

Lima, Ohio

I WAS THERE

8808 / ISBN 1-55673-021-7

Director's Notes

Characters

Doubt
Sorrow
Fear
Shame
Agony
Hate
Death

The above roles may be played by either men or women.

Props

A large cross
A blue spotlight
Seven candles

Playing Time

15 to 20 minutes

Music

"Were You There" — stanzas one through three are used during the drama and may be sung by the choir, the cast, or the congregation

Costuming

The service may be done without costume, but for best effect —
- all characters may wear black robes
- Death's head may be covered with a black hood
- Death's face may be highlighted and shadowed with light and dark make-up to give a death-like appearance

At rise: The sanctuary or auditorium is in darkness except for a single blue spotlight shining upon the chancel area or stage. A large cross is situated center stage. All characters enter left and exit right. Each carries a lighted candle and delivers his or her lines at the foot of the cross.

An alternative staging: None of the characters appear; only their voices are heard. These voices may be prerecorded or read from the wings or read from the choir loft. A large cross will occupy center stage. The seven candles will stand before the cross, either on a stand, or with the help of candle holders. As each character concludes his or her reading, an acolyte will extinguish a candle. A red spotlight may be added to be used alternately with the blue as each character speaks. A dimmer switch will allow these lights to fade into each other; they can even be made to pulsate with the speaking of each voice.

Either staging may be used during the sermon period of the Good Friday or any other worship service.

For most effective use, all other worship elements would precede the drama, so that following death's chilling speech the congregation may depart the worship area in silence, contemplating the enormity of what happened on this day.

I Was There

A Tenebrae Drama

The choir sings stanza one of "Were You There." ("Were you there when they crucified my Lord? . . .")

(A moment of silence follows the music. Enter Doubt from the left area of the chancel. Doubt is carrying a lighted candle. Doubt moves to center chancel area and stands at the foot of the cross facing the congregation.)

Doubt: Yes, I was there. I was there throughout the whole ordeal. *(pause)* But I was with him all along, right from the very beginning. I was with him in the wilderness. It was I who said, "If you be the Son of God, command that these stones be turned into bread." I was trying to convince him even then that he was a fool for believing that he was the Promised One, that he could have any effect on mankind and its destiny. But he was too strong for me then. He pushed me aside and began his work. But I am not to be dismissed that easily.

I followed him, and I attacked him again and again. But I went about it in a different way. I lashed out at him through his followers, those who came to hear his teachings. But again I failed. For his words warmed even the saddest of hearts, the blind received their sight, the lame walked, the dead returned to life.

But I was not to be out-done. I remained with his followers, and some of them I won. Through my efforts, some of them sought ways to trap him, discredit him, finally destroy him. I even worked my way into his circle of friends. I convinced one of them to betray him.

It took a lot of doing, but I had him where I wanted him. Because of me he said, "Let this cup pass from me." He was wondering if it had to be this way. He was doubting the climax of his mission. Yes, he knew that I was there. He had seen my presence in the faces of his followers, and once again he was feeling my attempt to surround him. *(pause)* I am Doubt *(pause)* and I was there. I was there, but I failed to destroy him. Once again he dismissed me with "Not my will, but thine be done." I was there, but he overcame me.

(Doubt extinguishes his candle and exits to the right of the chancel area. Sorrow enters from the left chancel area carrying a lighted candle. Sorrow stops at the foot of the cross and faces the congregation.)

Sorrow: I am Sorrow, and I was there; believe me I was there. I too attacked him with a vengeance. Many have fallen from the broken heart that I inflict, but not this one. Many have abandoned their goals, their hopes and dreams and chosen to live in self-pity. But again, he did not.

I did my best to defeat him. I reminded him constantly that he was unwanted in this world. I came to him as rejection, scorn, and ridicule. I tried to tell him that he was ridiculous for loving those who did not want him. I did my best, but I too failed.

Oh, I brought him plenty of heartache. I caused tears to fill his eyes on many occasions. But I couldn't break him; I couldn't even make him feel sorry for himself. *(He points to the cross.)* Even as he was struggling under this cross, his thoughts were on others. He said, "Daughters of Jerusalem, weep not for me, but for yourselves and your children . . ." I inflicted myself heavily upon him, but I couldn't destroy him.

(Sorrow extinguishes his candle and exits to the right of the chancel area. Fear enters from the left of the chancel area carrying a lighted candle. He stops at the foot of the cross and faces the congregation.)

Fear: I am Fear, and I was there. I literally surrounded him. I was with him in the garden. It was I who placed those great drops of sweat upon his forehead. I danced at him in the soldier's flaming torches, and I winked at him in the glistening of their swords and spears. I was present in every crack of the whip, and I was in the descending hammer that drove the nails through his hands and feet.

I was quite effective against his disciples. One of them denied ever knowing him, and they all ran like frightened children. I felt certain that I could destroy him. I longed to hear his voice beg for mercy. I longed to hear him promise to leave the country and abandon his foolish mission. I longed to hear this, but he remained silent. He refused to defend himself; he refused to retract anything that he had said. To be sure, he felt my presence, but I couldn't destroy him. I have failed.

(Fear extinguishes his candle and exits to the right of the chancel area.)

The choir sings stanza two of "Were You There." *("Were you there when they nailed him to the tree? . . .")*

(Enter Shame with lighted candle.)

Shame: I am Shame, and I too was there. Perhaps I failed because he was so used to me by now. I have been with him since his birth. I was the manger, the "king's" cradle. I was beside him in Nazareth when his friends and neighbors ran him out of town as a false prophet. I was in the sneering faces of his tormentors. I was the crown of thorns around his head. I was in the dice that the soldiers threw as they gambled for his clothing. I was in the sign that hung over his head. *(He points to the cross.)* I was in this cross itself, making it heavier as he carried it. I was there, but I could not break his spirit.

(Shame extinguishes candle and exits. Enter Agony with lighted candle.)

Agony: I was there, and I didn't let him forget my presence for one minute. I burned into his forehead with the thorns. I caused the sweat to trickle into his lash marks. I caused him to fall with weariness under the burden of his cross. Then I attacked him as brutally as I could. I ran across his body as the nails pierced his flesh. I caused his tongue to swell and burn with thirst. I beat upon him with the hot rays of the sun, causing his body to dehydrate.

As I was increasing my attack to its strongest, I leaped for joy, I thought I had succeeded. I heard him cry, "My God, My God, Why —" But my celebration was premature, for with his final words, he entrusted himself into his Father's hands. I am Agony, and I afflicted him greatly, but I too failed to destroy him.

(Agony extinguishes candle and exits. Enter Hate with lighted candle.)

Hate: I was there, and how I hated him. But you see, I hate everybody, for I am Hate. I do my job well, and I intended to destroy this teacher of love. And I tried, believe me I tried, but what were the results? He said, "Father, forgive —" I couldn't even make him hate that miserable wretch hanging beside him who asked for mercy. He wouldn't curse his tormentors, he wouldn't curse his Father, and, worst of all, he wouldn't even curse himself for going through with this foolish endeavor. Oh how I hated him, but I couldn't make him hate me. He is my greatest failure of all time.

(Hate extinguishes candle and exits.)

The choir sings stanza three of "Were You There." ("Were you there when they laid him in the tomb? . . .")

(Enter Death with lighted candle.)

Death: I was there, and, unlike my colleagues, I did not fail. Sooner or later every man falls beneath my power, and this man was no different from the rest. He made a lot of grand promises; he called himself the Resurrection and the Life. But today I proved that even he must submit to my eternal darkness. I proved that the peace, joy, and love that he spoke of will melt away in my presence. Tonight I reign victorious, and he lies defeated. He lies still like a crippled army at the end of a war. This war is over, and I have won. *(He pulls back his hood to reveal a skull-like face.)* I am Death, and the victory is mine.

(Death extinguishes candle and exits, laughing loudly in mocking and victorious tones.)

[A note in the worship folder may indicate that, in the tradition of Good Friday tenebrae services, the congregation leaves the worship area in silence. This signifies the fact that the service — and the story — is not finished, but will be completed on Easter morning.]

A Suggested Order of Worship

[In keeping with the somber mood of this day, no organ music is included and no hymns are sung. No offering is received. The drama concludes the service, after which, without benediction, the congregation departs in silence. A note in the worship folder may indicate to all that the service is not concluded, but finds its finish at worship on Easter Day.]

Invocation

Psalm 22 *(The psalm may be read in unison or responsively by the congregation, or by a reader)*

Litany

Pastor — Jesus, we have come to Calvary with you. We seek to know the agony you suffered there.

People — Hear our prayer, Lord Jesus.

Pastor — Teach us to endure, as you endured, the scorn of unbelievers and the torments of our enemies.

People — Hear our prayer, Lord Jesus.

Pastor — Save us from despair when we are circled round about.

People — Hear our prayer, Lord Jesus.

Pastor — Help us keep strong faith in you forever. When we falter, rescue us. When we forget your promises, refresh our memories. When we face death, be with us faithfully.

14

People — Hear our prayer, Lord Jesus.

[Silence]

The Death of Jesus

    I. Mark 8:34-37
[Silence]

    II. Mark 13:11-13
[Silence]

    III. Mark 14:43-46
[Silence]

    IV. Mark 14:55-59
[Silence]

    V. Mark 15:15-20
[Silence]

    VI. Mark 15:22-25
[Silence]

    VII. Mark 15:34-37
[Silence]

Receiving the Cross

Pastor — Receive the sign of Jesus' holy cross. *[The pastor makes the sign of the cross before the congregation.]* Take it again this day as a sign that you are his, participants in all his crucifixion means. Remember Jesus' agony, and your own death in Holy Baptism. Remember

how the cross of Jesus binds us to him and God's
promises — both in this life and for eternity.

People — **Amen.** *[They may cross themselves.]*

The Drama — "I Was There"